Sincerely, Yours Truly

Jamia Khan

BookLeaf
Publishing

India | USA | UK

Presentation by *BookLeaf Publishing*

Web: www.bookleafpub.com

E-mail: info@bookleafpub.com

ISBN: 9789357443609

First edition 2022

PREFACE

Pretending to be a poet brings on a blurred path. This compilation of poems is the start of many different journeys. The purpose is to write and share.

Sincerely

My poems can be abrupt, complex and messy
Just like my mentality
Leaving you perplexed and

Yours Truly

In the heart of our ghost town is the home which
weighs me down.
Hopes are engraved within the walls; they are
chipped and aged
Memories occupy the floors but they are
cluttered and cracked.

The vacancy of this house cannot be mistaken,
for the absence of life binds each brick
and my shell haunts every room.

The night train in our ghost town
is the emptiness which passes through me
and I'm tied to its tracks.

The end is walking through our halls
and painting our walls blue.

Our ghost town isn't flammable
but I stand in its ashes after the burn.
My shell reaches for the door;
the end knocks on the other side.

Our ghost town needs a heart
but I think this house of ours is burning down
too.

Dilemma

I tread lightly
as the path should be clear ahead of me.
The leaves fall and the wind blows.
The angel and devil who graced my shoulders
have nature in their stead.
She whispers in my ear,
the dualistic voices are hard to tell apart.

The more I listen, the further I stray.

I tread a path that has not been trodden before.
The two doors are insight.
Dilemma knocks on both.
I ponder the consequences of each path.
There is Death who is not known to discriminate
And Life who gambles with everyone's cards.

Those truths are engraved in front of me.
Dilemma knocks louder and will soon break in.
I can see it now but it's too late.

I'm running out of time.

To: Our Eternity

Dear Eternity,

We could stay alone together
Things with us couldn't be better
It's you and me, always and forever
In my ethereal dreams
They strain reality
Oh, darling, it's us for eternity.

Dumpster Showdown

6

I bring uninvited guests,
they linger and grow.
It's getting messy now.
I'm sorry that I can't throw them out.
This distorted vision of mine
keeps me as I am.
I'm a waste, but don't stop loving me
because you are too.
Instead,
Let's dance,
celebrate our dumpster showdown.

Bleed Blue

I stare at the balance in colours around us
The red on your hands contrasts the blue above
A rainbow in the sky brightens the rainy mood

Dry your eyes when you cry
Rainbows don't come from blue
Use the rain to paint the sky

Create colours just for you
Dilute the pain of red just for you
I'll bleed blue for you too

Destiny

The person I fear to be
is the one I already am.
I don't want to welcome my misery
but she's the only one who holds my hand.
If this is destiny,
then I don't understand.

Missing In Action

I do work like I always do
I study like I used to
Then what's so different?

There were a lot of memories
But they can't be made anymore
Why is that?

Where did it go?
That innocent smile
The hearty laughter

Something is missing
I don't remember what it is
When was it lost?

Sometimes

Sometimes I pretend to be a poet
I'll note down metaphors and phrases
But that does not change the fact
because I am not a poet

Sometimes I'll draw
but I'm no artist
Sometimes I'll cry
but I'm not known to be emotional

Sometimes I'll need you to tell me who I am
but who's to say?
I don't know
But sometimes I'll pretend

What's left of it

I want to see the whole world
that's why I need to work harder.

I'm not doing anything
but I want to see the whole world.

House of Cards

The end is near
I can see it crashing down

One mistake and it'll shatter
I tried to sustain it
But now it's strained
I'm holding on to the last pieces

I saw this coming
I couldn't stop it

It's all collapsing again
I'll try to put it all together again
Piece by piece
I'll try but it was already ruined

My house of cards.

118 Degrees

I have never been good at creating anything but
fire.
Bridges I set alight burn slowly.
The flames waltz across the wood,
slowly and steady,
You won't even realize it.
I'm learning to use lighters for candles
and to suffocate the unwanted flames.
I hope to reach the day
where the fire stops destroying
and instead illuminates.
Then I'll see
that the most precious things
are flammable too.

The Galaxy is Endless

I stare at the stars,
there are too many to count

Dreams are like stars, aren't they?
they are sporadic in position
but some have relatives in shape.

Like stars, they glow and burn.
And like stars, they die

There are some differences of course,
For the galaxy is endless
The stars extend until the end of time.
Our dreams, however,
are limited to our minds.

Wasted

Ages 7 to 16
Sunday to Monday
Dawn to dusk
How can it all be the same?

I'll start work right now
Just one more minute
One more post
Why can't I be faster?

I wish I started when I was younger
I'm behind now but I'll still get older
I didn't do anything today
Is this normal?

Every day is mundane
Squandering time I can't see
What did I do these past hours?
It was all wasted.

Ghosting

Our relationship goes past a screen
I feel you in my room
My closet is big enough for two

A dual breakfast is made
I hear the taunting laughter
Temperatures drop and I welcome a rifle

Seeing you everywhere and nowhere at once
I try to hit you somewhere vital
But the scope shows my reflection too

I can't breathe when we kiss
Yet your proximity is oxygen to me
This torture is because you're all I got

I live with a ghoul
Do you reside in my heart or my room?
Why haven't my buried feelings died with you?

Queen of Hearts

Strawberry conversations
can't melt the ice between us.

I drink gasoline and look away.
You're holding a match once again.

I can burn in your heart
as you dance with the flames

The red in my blood,
now intimidated by the red in your eyes

I break and burn from your touch
Do you enjoy the show?

Fall

Like the beautiful colours of leaves before they
break
I was at a high and that is keeping me low now
The flowers are blooming but my body is cold
Winter should be over now

Last year's petals have crumbled
They've fallen to my feet
What keeps me standing above them?
Like the dying leaves, I'll fall too

Let Go

Here at last,
I find myself at the final letter
Reading between the lines,
For one last time, our paths will split

Before saying goodbye, I'll need to let go
Our journeys are not parallel,
These paths will no longer connect
There is no finish line to the race we started.

To say goodbye, I'll have to let you know
Am I ready to let you go?
We can't avoid it any longer, time is catching up
to us

I need to let go.

www.ingramcontent.com/pod-product-compliance
Lightning Source LLC
Chambersburg PA
CBHW070738160726
48003CB00006BA/2559